KYLIAN MBAPPÉ

# KYLIAN MBAPPÉ

## ODYSSEYS

JORDAN FARGO

CREATIVE EDUCATION · CREATIVE PAPERBACKS

Published by Creative Education and Creative Paperbacks
P.O. Box 227, Mankato, Minnesota 56002
Creative Education and Creative Paperbacks are imprints of
The Creative Company
www.thecreativecompany.us

Design by Tom Morgan
Art direction by Blue Design

Images by Associated Press/Anthony Bibard/FEP, 16, 52, Dave Thompson, cover, 75; Dreamstime/Andre Ricardo Paes, 6, 39, Fabian Alberto De Ciria, 8, 11, 47, Hcazenave, 70–71, Marco Canoniero, 56, Marco Iacobucci, 61, Marta Fernandez, 2, Mitchell Gunn, 30, 33, 58, Stefan Ugljevarevic, 63, Vladyslav Moskovenko, 24, Wirestock, 51; Getty Images/Agence Nice Presse, 19, Alex Livesey - Danehouse, 4–5, Cui Nan/China News Service, 48, JOEL SAGET, 69, Sven Hoppe/picture alliance, 64; Wikimedia Commons/Jos. Lantz, 12, Kremlin.ru, 28–29, Narelav, 20, Sandro Halank, 66, Эдгар Брещанов, 27

Every effort has been made to contact copyright holders for material reproduced in this book. Any omissions will be rectified in subsequent printings if notice is given to the publisher.

Copyright © 2026 Creative Education, Creative Paperbacks
International copyright reserved in all countries. No part of this book may be reproduced in any form without written permission from the publisher.

Library of Congress Cataloging-in-Publication Data
Names: Fargo, Jordan author
Title: Kylian Mbappé / Jordan Fargo.
Description: Mankato, Minnesota : Creative Education and Creative Paperbacks, [2026] | Series: Odysseys in sports: soccer stars | Includes bibliographical references and index. | Audience: Ages 12-15 | Audience: Grades 7-9 | Summary: "Kylian Mbappé, the Real Madrid forward who captained France to its 2018 World Cup victory, dazzles soccer fans with his speed and dribbling. This action-packed biography for early high schooler readers kicks up interest in his stellar career"– Provided by publisher.
Identifiers: LCCN 2025018192 (print) | LCCN 2025018193 (ebook) | ISBN 9798895811399 library binding | ISBN 9798896800927 paperback | ISBN 9798895812655 ebook
Subjects: LCSH: Mbappé, Kylian, 1998-Juvenile literature | Soccer players–France–Biography–Juvenile literature
Classification: LCC GV942.7.M3928 F37 2026 (print) | LCC GV942.7.M3928 (ebook) | DDC 796.334092 [B]-dc23/eng/20250617
LC record available at https://lccn.loc.gov/2025018192
LC ebook record available at https://lccn.loc.gov/2025018193

Printed in the United States

Mbappé and teammates celebrate France's win in the 2018 World Cup.

## CONTENTS

**Introduction** . . . . . . . . . . . . . . . . . . . . . . . 9

**Birth of a Star** . . . . . . . . . . . . . . . . . . . . . 13

Sibling Soccer Stars. . . . . . . . . . . . . . . . . . 20

**Rise to Success** . . . . . . . . . . . . . . . . . . . . 31

Many Down, One to Go. . . . . . . . . . . . . . 39

A FIFA Fan Favorite. . . . . . . . . . . . . . . . . 43

**Top of the World** . . . . . . . . . . . . . . . . . . 44

Eyes on the Prize . . . . . . . . . . . . . . . . . . 51

All Eyes on Mbappé. . . . . . . . . . . . . . . . . 54

**Building His Legacy** . . . . . . . . . . . . . . . 59

Helping Others. . . . . . . . . . . . . . . . . . . . 69

Business Success . . . . . . . . . . . . . . . . . 70

**Selected Bibliography** . . . . . . . . . . . . . 76

**Glossary** . . . . . . . . . . . . . . . . . . . . . . . . 77

**Websites** . . . . . . . . . . . . . . . . . . . . . . . . 79

**Index** . . . . . . . . . . . . . . . . . . . . . . . . . . 80

KYLIAN MBAPPÉ

# Introduction

The 2022 **FIFA** World Cup final between France and Argentina would go down as one of the greatest finals in soccer (football) history. Argentina, led by Lionel Messi, was on a quest to win the title for their captain. It took a 2–0 lead with goals from Messi and Ángel Di María. But France wasn't done yet, and neither was its 23-year-old **forward**, Kylian Mbappé. In a stunning turn of

**OPPOSITE:** Mbappé was France's hero during the exciting 2022 World Cup final against Argentina.

events in the second half, Mbappé scored twice within mere minutes, once on a penalty, tying the match at 2–2 and forcing extra time.

Extra time brought more drama. Messi struck again, putting Argentina back in front. But Mbappé still wasn't finished! In the final minutes of extra time, he stepped up again to score another penalty, bringing the score to 3–3. This feat marked only the second **hat-trick** in a World Cup final, the first since Geoff Hurst in 1966.

The climax came in the **penalty shootout**. Argentina triumphed 4–2, but Mbappé's heroics were unforgettable. His three goals in the final brought his tournament total to eight, and he edged out Messi to win the **Golden Boot** as the tournament's top scorer. Despite his team's loss, there was no doubt that Mbappé's future was bright, and he had established himself as an unforgettable player.

Mbappé and Messi embrace during the 2022 World Cup final.

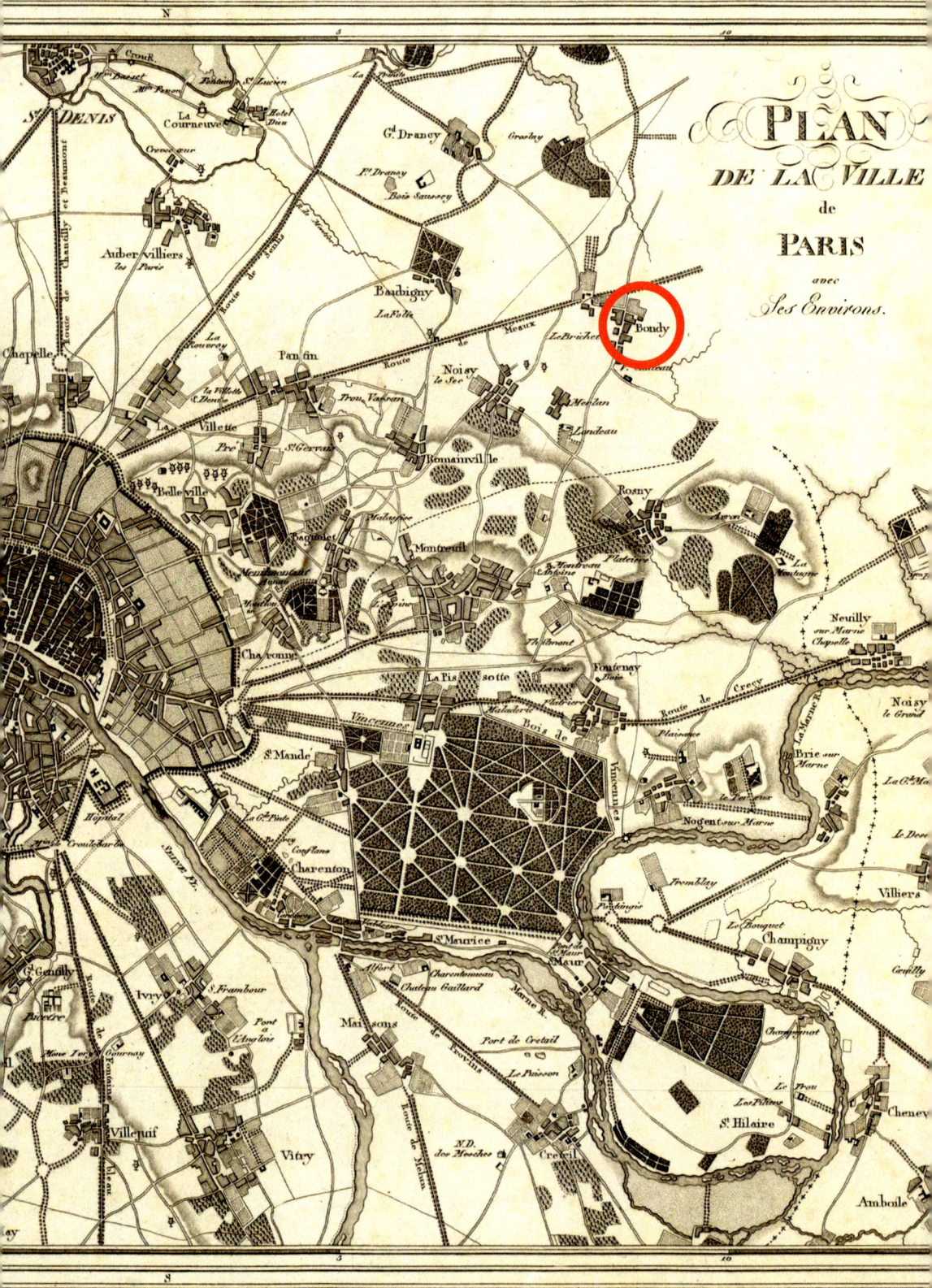

KYLIAN MBAPPÉ

## Birth of a Star

Kylian Mbappé is one of the most exciting players in soccer, and his journey to the top didn't just happen by chance. It came from a mix of hard work, natural skill, and a passion for the game that started when he was very young. Born on December 20, 1998, in Paris, France, Mbappé has followed an inspiring path from playing in his neighborhood to becoming a world-class player.

**OPPOSITE:** Mbappé grew up in a suburb of Paris called Bondy.

Mbappé's story starts with his family. His dad, Wilfried Mbappé, was a soccer player who later became a coach. His mom, Fayza Lamari, played handball. Growing up in a household filled with athletes, Mbappé was always surrounded by sports. The Mbappé home was buzzing with the excitement of sports competitions.

Wilfried played a key role in Kylian's growth. As a coach, he knew what it took to succeed and shared that knowledge with his son. He took Kylian to soccer fields, encouraging him to work hard, practice, and always give his best effort. This support helped Kylian build a strong mindset and a powerful desire to improve.

Kylian grew up in Bondy, a suburb of Paris that wasn't famous for producing soccer stars. But the streets and parks of Bondy were where he first trained. He played soccer with his friends, dreaming of becoming a pro one day. Even then, Mbappé's talent was clear. He was fast, skilled with the ball, and had an amazing knack for making **defenders** look foolish with his **dribbling**.

At just six years old, Mbappé joined his first soccer club, AS Bondy. There, he quickly became known as one of the best players in his age group. His speed was a huge advantage, allowing him to outrun defenders, and his quick footwork helped him maneuver around them easily. But what really made Mbappé special

Clairefontaine players in 2024

was his smart play on the field. He had a natural understanding of the game.

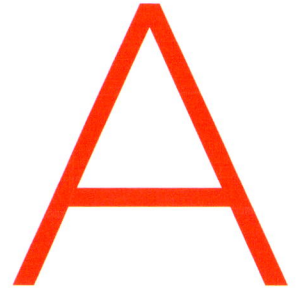At the age of 13, Mbappé took a big leap by moving to the Clairefontaine academy. It was a significant change for him, but he was eager to show what he could do. Clairefontaine is famous for its rigorous training and high expectations, but Mbappé embraced the challenge. The academy helped him sharpen his technical skills and taught him valuable lessons about discipline, teamwork, and handling pressure.

While at Clairefontaine, Mbappé trained alongside some of the best young talents in France, but he really stood out. His speed and skill made him a star during practices and games. It was obvious that he had the potential to achieve great things. He spent several years there, growing as both a player and a person.

After leaving Clairefontaine, Mbappé joined AS Monaco, one of the top clubs in France's **Ligue 1**. His rise at Monaco was rapid. He began playing for the senior team at just 16 years old, which is unusual

Mbappé playing for AS Monaco in 2016

## Sibling Soccer Stars

Kylian isn't the only member of the Mbappé family to make waves in the soccer world. Ethan Mbappé, born on December 29, 2006, is already a professional player! He is a midfielder in the French Ligue 1. Ethan started out with local side AS Bondy in 2015, before moving to Paris Saint-Germain's (PSG's) youth team in 2017. In 2024, he signed a three-year contract with Ligue 1 club Lille, his first professional contract. "At my age, staying in France was the best option to grow. I think Lille was the best project. It's one of the best clubs in France," Ethan said after the move.

since most players are still in the youth teams at that age. He made his debut for Monaco in 2015 and quickly made a significant impact.

In his first full season with Monaco, Mbappé scored in nearly every match. His speed and dribbling skills made him a nightmare for defenders. But it wasn't just his ball skills that impressed everyone; it was also his smart play and awareness on the field. He always seemed to be in the right spot, creating chances for his teammates while scoring goals himself.

During the 2016–2017 season, Mbappé's talent shined. Monaco won the Ligue 1 title that year, and Mbappé was a key player in their success. He ended the season with 15 goals in the league and was named French Player of the Year, at just 18 years old. His outstanding performances not only helped Monaco secure their first league title in 17 years but also made Mbappé one of the most wanted young players in Europe.

By the summer of 2017, Mbappé was the talk of the town among some of the biggest soccer clubs in the world. Teams like Real Madrid and Barcelona were rumored to want him, but it was Paris Saint-Germain (PSG) that ended up signing him. PSG is one of the wealthiest and most influential clubs in Europe, and they were excited to bring Mbappé on board to help them chase major trophies, including the **UEFA** Champions League title.

In August 2017, Mbappé made the switch to PSG. He joined on a loan deal which allowed PSG to buy him permanently the next year. The deal was worth an eye-popping 180 million euros (around $190 million), making him the second-most expensive player in the world at that time, just behind Neymar.

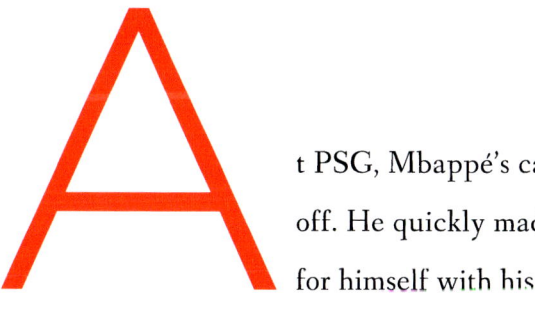

At PSG, Mbappé's career took off. He quickly made a name for himself with his goals and **assists**. His speed and skill at getting past defenders

Mbappé was one of the youngest players to be selected for the French national team.

made him one of the most thrilling players in the French league. But Mbappé wasn't just a goal-scorer, he also worked hard for the team, helping on defense and setting up his teammates for goals. In his first season with PSG, Mbappé played a big part in helping the team win the French league title. He scored 13 goals in league play.

bappé's talent was recognized beyond his club. His outstanding performances also got him a spot on the French national team, where he became one of the youngest players ever to represent his country.

He made his debut for France in March 2017 when he was only 18 years old. His speed and skills made him a dangerous player in international games, and he quickly became a regular on the team.

In 2018, Mbappé got the chance of a lifetime: to play for France in the FIFA World Cup. At just 19 years old, he played a key role in helping France win the tournament. He scored four goals, including one in the final against Croatia, and was named the Best Young Player of the tournament. He became the youngest player to score in a World Cup final since Pelé in 1958. This was a historic moment in his career, one that he would always remember. It was just the beginning of a highly successful soccer career.

Mbappé was named Best Young Player of the 2018 World Cup.

Mbappé celebrates winning the 2018 World Cup with the France.

KYLIAN MBAPPÉ

## Rise to Success

At PSG, Mbappé was already one of the most exciting players in Ligue 1, but he wanted to achieve even more. The 2018–2019 season was a standout for him, as he became PSG's top scorer with 33 goals, breaking several club records along the way. His speed and skill made it tough for defenders, and his partnership with Neymar and

**OPPOSITE:** Mbappé broke many club records with PSG.

Edinson Cavani created one of the most dangerous attacking teams in Europe.

While Mbappé was shining in Ligue 1, PSG had their eyes set on winning the UEFA Champions League, the top club competition in Europe. That season, the team made it far in the knockout rounds but faced a shocking defeat against Manchester United in the Round of 16. The loss was tough. It showed that PSG still needed to improve to compete with the best teams in Europe.

UEFA Champions League Round of 16

The 2019–2020 season was a big moment for Mbappé. PSG, coached by Thomas Tuchel, made it to the Champions League final for the first time ever. Mbappé was a key player, scoring important goals and proving he could handle the pressure of big games. Unfortunately, PSG lost to Bayern Munich 1–0 in the final. It was tough to take, but it also showed how much the team had improved.

PSG dominated Ligue 1, finishing at the top, and Mbappé scored goals easily. By the end of the season, at just 21 years old, he had scored 18 goals in Ligue 1 and was named Player of the Year. Even with these personal awards, Mbappé was focused on the bigger goal—winning the Champions League with PSG and becoming an even better player.

As he grew older, he would always remember that soccer is a game, and that every player is still a child at heart with a lifelong passion for the game. "We tend to forget it, but we're eternally children when we play football," Mbappé said. "The level at which we play the game changes, but the mentality doesn't. The passion is constant through the years."

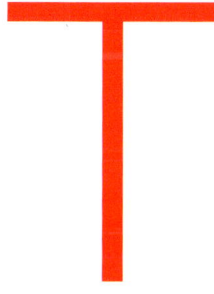

The 2020–2021 season was a major turning point for Mbappé. By then, he had become PSG's most important player, a role he would continue to strengthen in the following seasons. Mbappé was now the main player in PSG's attack, often leading them to victory with his goals and assists.

One of his standout moments was during PSG's quarterfinal match in the Champions League against Barcelona. In the first leg, Mbappé dazzled at the Camp Nou, Barça's stadium, scoring an incredible hat-trick that put PSG in a strong position. His speed and finishing skills were amazing, and it looked like he couldn't be stopped.

PSG had a pretty up-and-down season in their home league. Mbappé played well, but the team struggled, especially with tough competition from teams like Lille and Lyon. In the end, PSG ended up in second place, losing the title to Lille, which surprised many fans. Still, Mbappé shone individually, scoring 27 goals and becoming the top scorer in Ligue 1 for the third time. He could change the game all by himself.

Even with the challenges in Ligue 1 and the Champions League, Mbappé's reputation kept getting better. He was known for stepping up in crucial moments and was a key player for PSG during tough games. His leadership grew stronger, and he often wore the captain's armband for both France and PSG when senior players were missing.

By the 2021–2022 season, Mbappé was recognized as one of the best players in the world. At just 23, he was already a leader in Ligue 1 and for the French national team. That season, he helped PSG win another Ligue 1 title, scoring 28 goals and earning the title of Ligue 1's Player of the Year again. His amazing performances made him the star of PSG's offense, with Neymar and Lionel Messi often playing behind him.

However, PSG still had a tough time in the Champions League. In the 2021–2022 Champions League, PSG was knocked out in the Round of 16 by Real Madrid, another disappointing moment for the club. The loss showed that PSG still had work to do to compete with the best teams in Europe. While Mbappé's talent had

# Many Down, One to Go

Mbappé has many ground-breaking achievements. His four World Cup final goals, across two finals (2018 and 2022), are an all-time record. He is the youngest Frenchman to win the FIFA World Cup (in 2018) and the youngest player in the world to score hat-trick in a World Cup final (in 2022). Mbappé was Ligue 1 Player of the Year five times and top goal scorer six times. Despite these accomplishments, he has yet to earn a **Ballon d'Or**, the award given to the year's best professional player.

taken PSG far, the dream of winning the Champions League was still out of reach.

Mbappé's future became a hot topic during this time. With his contract ending in the summer of 2022, everyone was buzzing about where he might go next. Real Madrid had been interested in him for a long time, and many thought that would be his next stop. However, in May 2022, Mbappé surprised everyone by announcing he would stay at PSG. He signed a new three-year deal.

Mbappé was also making waves with the French national team. He was stepping up as a leader crucial to the team's success. During the UEFA Euro 2020, which took place in 2021 because of the COVID-19 pandemic, Mbappé was one of France's standout players. Unfortunately, the tournament ended badly for the defending champions when they lost to Switzerland in a nail-biting penalty shootout in the Round of 16.

Despite this setback, Mbappé's reputation as one of the best players in the world kept growing. He scored many goals for France in World Cup qualifiers and friendly matches, solidifying his role as the team's star. His leadership and drive to win shone through in every game, and he was seen as someone who could handle pressure in crucial moments, just like he did in the 2018 World Cup.

"The desire to win, to go beyond the limits of what is possible, and to do great things is deeply ingrained in me. I think I owe it to the education and guidance I received both on and off the pitch, which helped me to build myself as a player and as a man," he said.

As the 2022 World Cup drew near, Kylian Mbappé was one of the most exciting players to watch. Having already won the World Cup in 2018 and

## A FIFA Fan Favorite

Many young soccer players have dreamed of making the front cover of FIFA, the hit soccer video game series. Mbappé got his wish when he was featured in the front cover of FIFA 21. He was also the cover star for FIFA 22 and 23, a special hat-trick. "Representing all three editions of the FIFA game is a dream come true," he said. "This game has been part of my life since my childhood and continues to be something I enjoy sharing with my friends every day." The record for most covers in a row belongs to Wayne Rooney (FIFA 06 to 12).

achieved great things at the club level, he was ready to shine again on the world stage. His performances leading up to the tournament only added to his impressive legacy, and fans everywhere were eager to see what he would accomplish next. From 2018 to 2022, Mbappé kept evolving, both as a player and a leader.

KYLIAN MBAPPÉ

# Top of the World

By the end of the 2022 season, Mbappé had scored 28 goals in Ligue 1, once again finishing as the league's top scorer. His pace and ability to get past defenders were as sharp as ever, but it was his improvement in other areas—like his vision, decision-making, and passing—that made him even more dangerous. His link-up play with Messi and Neymar had reached another level. Together, they formed one of the most lethal attacking trios in European football.

In addition to his goals in Ligue 1, Mbappé also played a key role in PSG's run in the UEFA Champions League. Though PSG's goal of winning the Champions League still eluded the team, he delivered some memorable performances in the knockout rounds. His speed and skill created many opportunities, and while PSG was knocked out in the Round of 16 by Bayern Munich, Mbappé's performances only added to his reputation.

Mbappé's performances at PSG were phenomenal, but it was on the world stage—at the 2022 FIFA World Cup in Qatar—where his greatness truly shone. For Mbappé, the 2022 World Cup was nothing short of a dream. He had already been the star of the 2018 World Cup, and expectations were high for him to repeat his magic. Despite dealing with some injuries leading up to the tournament, Mbappé was ready to go once the tournament kicked off.

From the very first match, Mbappé set the tone for what would be an unforgettable tournament. France's opening game against Australia was a perfect example of his ability to dominate a match. In the first half, France found themselves 1–0 down, but Mbappé scored a quick-fire **brace** in the second half to lead France to a 4–1 victory. His goals were a perfect display of his speed,

France's goal against Australia in the opening game of the 2022 World Cup

Mbappé demonstrates his remarkable skills in spectacular aerial action.

composure, and clinical finishing. The way he dribbled past defenders with ease, then finished with precision, was something only a few players in the world could do.

The next game for France came against Denmark. Once again, Mbappé was the star. After helping set up a goal and providing a constant threat down the left wing, Mbappé helped seal a 2–1 victory. With two wins from their first two matches, France secured their place in the knockout stages. But it wasn't just the results that were impressive—it was the way Mbappé was playing. He was leading the French attack and showing the world that he had become one of the best players to ever grace the World Cup stage.

I n the Round of 16, France faced Poland, and Mbappé delivered a performance for the ages. In a 3–1 victory, Mbappé scored two goals—each more beautiful than the other. His first goal was a long-range shot that flew past the Polish goalkeeper with incredible power and precision. His second goal, which sealed the victory, was a stunning volley that left fans around the world in awe. With five goals by the time the quarter-

## Eyes on the Prize

Mbappé was on the cover of *Sports Illustrated's* December 2022 issue and on *Time* magazine's "The 100 Most Influential People of 2023" list. But he was less concerned with individual awards than with winning the team prize. During the 2022 World Cup, he said, "I didn't come here to win the **Golden Ball** or Golden Boot. If I win it, of course I am going to be happy, but that's not why I'm here. The only objective for me is to win the World Cup."

Mbappé celebrates a goal in the 2022 World Cup Round of 16 match against Poland.

finals came around, Mbappé had more goals than any other player, even Lionel Messi. But his job wasn't done.

The quarterfinals saw France face England, a match filled with drama and high expectations. England, led by Harry Kane and with a strong defense, was one of the toughest teams in the tournament. But once again, Mbappé stepped up when his team needed him most. Although he didn't score in this match, Mbappé was a constant threat to England's defense. His pace and dribbling caused problems for the defenders throughout

## All Eyes on Mbappé

The 2022 World Cup in Qatar was one of the most popular televised sporting events in history. A record-breaking 5 billion people tuned in to watch the tournament at one point or another. That's more than half of the entire population on Earth! Nearly 1.5 billion people across the globe tuned in for the championship final match between France and Argentina alone. Billions of people also watched and engaged with the 2022 World Cup on social media.

the match. When France won 2–1, it was clear that Mbappé had played a huge role in keeping the English defense on edge.

In the semifinals, France faced Morocco, the first African nation to ever reach the World Cup semifinals. Though Mbappé didn't score, his ability to create space and deliver key passes was crucial in France's 2–0 victory. It was clear by now that France's road to the final was paved by Mbappé's performances.

The dramatic final was on December 18, 2022, just two days before Mbappé's 24th birthday. Some 1.5 billion fans tuned in to watch France face Argentina. The excitement was palpable, especially with Mbappé and Messi on the field.

Argentina's confidence was high. Its goalkeeper Emiliano Martínez stated, "People say the favorites are France. But we have the greatest player of all time."

Argentina triumphed 4–2 on penalties, but not before Mbappé's superb scoring sent the game first into overtime and then into penalties. Having singlehandedly kept France alive throughout the tournament, and especially against Argentina, Mbappé secured the

Mbappé has been gracious acknowledging rivals, such as soccer great Lionel Messi.

Golden Boot as the tournament's top scorer. As French president Emmanuel Macron stood with him on the sidelines after Argentina's victory, it was clear that Mbappé had made an impact on not just France, but the entire world.

The Golden Ball, the most prestigious individual award in the World Cup, went to Messi. Mbappé graciously acknowledged Messi's deserving win. "I knew he would win it the night of the World Cup final," Mbappé said after the game. "Messi deserves it. If he wins the World Cup, he has to win the Golden Ball. He is one of the best in history, if not the best."

KYLIAN MBAPPÉ

# Building His Legacy

Following the 2022 World Cup, Kylian Mbappé's future at Paris Saint-Germain was in the spotlight. Leading up to the World Cup, rumors had been swirling about a potential move to Real Madrid. However, in May 2022, Mbappé made a surprising announcement that he would stay at PSG. He signed a new contract that would keep him at the club for three more years. This decision was a game changer, as it signified that PSG

**OPPOSITE:** Mbappé signed a three-year contract extension with PSG in 2022.

had their star player locked down for the future, while also making Mbappé the center of their plans.

bappé's decision to stay at PSG was strategic. The new contract came with significant promises, including a larger role in the club's operations and a more central role in their quest for Champions League glory. For Mbappé, the challenge was clear: continue to perform at the highest level for PSG and lead the team to their first-ever Champions League title.

Mbappé in action during a 2021 match between France and Belgium

# "HIS ABILITY TO CREATE CHANCES AND FINISH CLINICALLY MADE HIM ALMOST UNSTOPPABLE."

In the 2022–2023 season, Mbappé once again showed his unmatched abilities on the pitch. He had already cemented himself as PSG's best player, but in the aftermath of the World Cup, he seemed to play with even more confidence and hunger. In Ligue 1, Mbappé continued his domination, finishing the 2022–2023 season as the league's top scorer with 29 goals. His ability

Mbappé and Neymar

to create chances and finish clinically made him almost unstoppable. The 24-year-old had become the focal point of PSG's attack, with Messi and Neymar playing in supporting roles.

But while his individual performances were exceptional, the real test for PSG and Mbappé was in the Champions League. For years, PSG had been one of the

Mbappé reacts during a PSG game.

most powerful teams in Europe, but they had not been able to secure the coveted Champions League trophy. In the 2022–2023 campaign, PSG made it to the Round of 16, where they faced Bayern Munich in a matchup that would determine whether they could finally break through and make a run for the title.

Despite Mbappé's best efforts, PSG was once again eliminated by Bayern Munich in a heartbreaking 3–2 **aggregate loss**. While the disappointment was evident, Mbappé's performances were still the bright spots in a

Mbappé's leadership was crucial to PSG and France.

tough season for the club. His leadership on the field was undeniable, and it was clear that he was the one player who could take PSG to new heights—if only the team could fully support him in the way that he deserved.

In the months following the 2022 World Cup, Mbappé became the undisputed leader of the French national team. Despite the loss to Argentina in the final,

# "MBAPPÉ WAS NOW SEEN AS THE PLAYER WHO WOULD CARRY THEM FORWARD."

the French squad still had one of the world's most talented rosters, and Mbappé was now seen as the player who would carry them forward. In the UEFA Euro 2024 qualification campaign, Mbappé had an impressive showing, scoring several key goals.

Off the field, Mbappé stepped up as a leader in the French team. With veteran players like goalkeeper Hugo Lloris retiring, he took on more responsibility, guiding the team through the ups and downs of international competition. He became a mentor for younger teammates while keeping the winning spirit alive, which was essential for their success.

The 2023–2024 season was a fresh start for PSG, as they aimed to build a team that could finally win the Champions League. Mbappé's importance to the team grew even more. In the early part of the season, he was in great shape, scoring several goals and being a key player in the team's offense. However, as the season went on, PSG faced challenges in the Champions League, especially against Borussia Dortmund and AC Milan.

While Mbappé played exceptionally well, PSG's inconsistency

## Helping Others

Mbappé tries to help others, especially disadvantaged children. After winning the World Cup in 2018, he donated his reported $500,000 award to charity. He gave the money to Premiers de Cordée, an organization that offers sports opportunities to children who are hospitalized or have disabilities. When Mbappé was only 21 years old, he started Inspired by KM, an effort to help 98 children from Paris fulfill their dreams. Mbappé said he would help the children to pursue whatever path they choose. "We will support them until their working lives begin," he said.

## Business Success

Mbappé is not only a soccer star but also a businessman. After his success at the 2018 World Cup, Adidas, Puma, and Nike wanted to sign him up to promote their merchandise. In 2019, he signed a ten-year contract with Nike said to be worth about 160 million euro ($175 million). Mbappé enjoys his business success. He is a car enthusiast and owns many luxury cars. The most famous are a Ferrari 488 Pista and a Mercedes V Class.

and lack of depth in important positions became clear. Despite his strong performance in the group stage, PSG struggled again in the knockout rounds, leading to another disappointing exit. The team's failure in Europe became a hot topic, and once more, the Champions League title seemed just out of reach.

Even though PSG did not reach their dream of winning in Europe, Mbappé shined brightly in France. His performances in Ligue 1 were amazing, and he became the clear leader of PSG once Neymar and Messi left in the summer of 2023. In Ligue 1, Mbappé helped PSG win another championship, showcasing his goal-scoring skills and making important assists. He was Ligue 1's top scorer for a record sixth time, with 27 goals. His steady performances were key to PSG's continued success in French football.

In June 2024, Mbappé unexpectedly announced he would move to Real Madrid in **La Liga**. He was quite excited about the move. "I will leave my country for the first time," Mbappé said. "It's going to be an amazing experience, and I can't wait to be in my new club. I want to win trophies. When you speak about football, [it's about] winning trophies, being with new teammates."

Although other top soccer stars like Messi had different ideas in mind for the Frenchman, they still supported his decision to go to Madrid. "I prefer that you go

**OPPOSITE** Mbappé celebrates scoring Real Madrid's first goal in a Champions League match against Manchester City in 2025.

to Barça," Messi reportedly said to Mbappé. "But if you want to go to Madrid, do it, you deserve a real winning project." Ultimately, Mbappé knew that he was making the smartest decision for himself professionally, even if some people didn't support it. As one of the world's most skilled and popular soccer players, he did what he had to do to keep the momentum going.

With the 2026 World Cup not too far away, Mbappé was set to further enhance his legacy. Kylian Mbappé will be remembered not just for his amazing soccer skills and performances, but also for how he always stays focused on the future. As a role model for young athletes and a representative of the sport of soccer, Mbappé's influence will continue to reach far beyond the game.

# Selected Bibliography

Ashby, Kevin, and Michael Part. *Kylian Mbappé the Golden Boy (Soccer Stars Series)*. Sole Books, 2024.

Coninx, Harry. *Mbappé (Tales from the Pitch)*. Leapfrog Press, 2023.

FIFA World History Museum. *The Official History of the FIFA World Cup*. Welbeck Publishing, 2024.

Jökulsson, Illugi. *Stars of World Soccer*. 4th ed. Abbeville Kids, 2023.

*Kylian Mbappé: The Unstoppable Rise*. London: Icon Books, 2020.

Lisi, Clemente A. *The FIFA World Cup: A History of the Planet's Biggest Sporting Event*. Rowman & Littlefield Publishers, 2022.

Spragg, Iain. *Kylian Mbappé: The Ultimate Fan Book*. London: Carlton Books, 2018.

Tran, Kerry. *Kylian Mbappé: The Journey of the Boy Who Became a Champion*. 2024.

United Library. *Kylian Mbappé: The Biography of the French Professional Football Star, Leadership and Legacy*. United Library, 2021.

Van Cleave, Ryan G. *Kylian Mbappé: Soccer Icon (Sports Illustrated Kids Stars of Sports)*. Capstone Press, 2024.

Wahl, Grant. *Masters of Modern Soccer: How the World's Best Play the Twenty-First-Century Game*. Crown, 2019.

# Glossary

**aggregate loss**  a loss that occurs when a team has a lower total score than another team after two or more games, usually in a knockout round

**assist**  a pass to another player that leads directly to a goal

**Ballon d'Or**  an award given to the world's best professional soccer player of the year

**brace**  when a player scores two goals in a single match

**Clairefontaine**  one of the best-known and prestigious soccer academies in the world

**defender**  a player whose main role is to stop the opposing team from scoring a goal

**draw**  when both teams have scored the same number of goals after the end of playing time

**dribbling**  the technique of controlling and advancing the soccer ball past opponents while moving with it

**FIFA**  stands for Fédération Internationale de Football Association (French), the governing body for soccer national teams and clubs around the world

**forward**  a player whose main role is to score goals for his team

| | |
|---|---|
| **Golden Ball** | an award given to the best player in the FIFA World Cup |
| **Golden Boot** | an award given to the player who scores the most goals in the FIFA World Cup |
| **hat-trick** | when a player scores three goals in a single game |
| **La Liga** | the top men's professional soccer division in Spain |
| **Ligue 1** | the top men's professional soccer division in France |
| **penalty shootout** | a tie-breaking method to determine which team wins a match that cannot end in a draw. Each team has five shots, and the team that successfully makes more kicks is declared the winner. |
| **UEFA** | stands for Union of European Football Associations, the governing body for European national teams and clubs |

# Websites

**FIFA World Cup Qatar 2022™**
https://www.fifa.com/en/tournaments/mens/worldcup/qatar2022
Relive exciting matches and stellar performances from the 2022 World Cup in Qatar, including all of Mbappé's eight goals.

**Kylian Mbappé – Real Madrid**
https://www.espn.com/soccer/player/_/id/231388/kylian-Mbappé
The official ESPN player page for Kylian Mbappé includes lifetime stats, recent match performances, upcoming matches, and more.

**Kylian Mbappé**
https://kylianMbappé.com/en/
Kylian Mbappé's official website features performances, records and achievements, official partners and sponsors, and an online apparel shop.

**US National Soccer Players**
https://ussoccerplayers.com/soccer-terms
Learn more about soccer players, key terms, and other information for new soccer fans.

# Index

2018 FIFA World Cup, 26, 27, 28, 39, 41, 42, 46, 69, 70
2022 FIFA World Cup, 9, 10, 39, 41, 42, 46, 47, 50, 51, 52, 54, 57, 59, 62, 66
2026 FIFA World Cup, 74
AC Milan, 68
Adidas, 70
Argentina (national team), 9, 10, 54, 55, 57, 66
AS Bondy, 15, 20
AS Monaco, 18, 19, 21, 22
Ballon d'Or, 39
Bayern Munich, 34, 45, 65
Bondy (Paris suburb), 15
brace, 46
Camp Nou, 36
Cavani, Edinson, 32
Clairefontaine, 16, 17, 18
COVID-19 pandemic, 41
Di María, Ángel, 9
Euro 2020, 41
FIFA video game series, 43
France (national team), 9, 24, 25, 26, 28, 38, 41, 46, 47, 49, 50, 53, 54, 55, 57, 61, 66, 67
Golden Ball, 51, 57
Golden Boot, 10, 51, 57
hat-trick, 10, 36, 39, 43
Hurst, Geoff, 10
Inspired by KM, 69
Kane, Harry, 53
La Liga, 73
leadership, 37, 38, 41, 43, 66, 67, 72
Lille, 20, 37
Ligue 1, 18, 20, 22, 31, 32, 34, 37, 38, 39, 44, 45, 62, 72, 73
Lloris, Hugo, 67
Manchester City, 75
Manchester United, 32
Mbappé, Ethan, 20
Messi, Lionel, 9, 10, 11, 38, 44, 53, 55, 56, 57, 63, 72, 73, 74

Morocco (national team), 54
Neymar, 23, 31, 38, 44, 63, 72
Nike, 70
Paris Saint-Germain (PSG), 20, 22, 23, 25, 31, 32, 34, 35, 36, 37, 38, 40, 45, 46, 59, 60, 62, 63, 64, 65, 66, 68, 72, 73
Pelé, 26
penalty shootout, 10, 41
Poland (national team), 50, 52
Premiers de Cordée, 69
Real Madrid, 22, 38, 40, 59, 73, 74, 75
Rooney, Wayne, 43
Round of 16 (World Cup), 32, 33, 38, 41, 45, 50, 52, 65
scoring record, 39, 73
*Sports Illustrated*, 51
*Time* magazine, 51
Tuchel, Thomas, 34
UEFA Champions League, 22, 32, 33, 34, 36, 37, 38, 40, 45, 60, 63, 65, 68, 72, 75